Back To The Basics

Simple Secrets For Living In Victory

TOYIN OKUTINYANG

Back to the Basics

Contents

I so appreciate this book, as its message is a reminder for all ministers and congregants to get back to the basics of scriptural teachings. With so many itching ear messages around the body of Christ today, it is refreshing to hear a clear, unadulterated challenge to get back to the basics. These are foundational biblical truths that will bring success and stability to each one of us when applied through grace and faith in our lives.

Rev. Richard Ciaramitaro
President, Open Bible Faith Fellowship of Canada
(OBFF)

Christianity is not that convoluted. At the end of the day it's just about a set of principles. To underscore that point our Lord Jesus reduced 613 commandments to two: love God, love your fellow man. This book tows the same rope.

What Toyin has done is reduce the Christian walk to just a few guidelines everyone can follow. She's showing us

Christianity is not hard after all. This book is about the simplicity of faith. And it's written so simply!

Leke Alder

Strategy, Policy & Brand Consultant

Principal, Alder Consulting

Lagos, Nigeria & London, England

Acknowledgements

Thank you Jesus for EVERYTHING! My Lord and my God, Your love, mercy and marvelous help alone has made me all that I am in You.

Thank you my dearest husband Inyang for three decades of your unfailing love, constant prayers and for always believing in me. Together we've taken and we're still taking territories for Jesus!

Thank you my beloved children Annikan, Adian and Achi – you are my reward from God!

Thank you my cherished Mom and Dad, whose love and presence I'm still blessed to enjoy. You raised me and released me to be all that I am and can.

Thank you my faithful friends who have walked with me at different stages along this journey of life. You know yourselves. Thank you for the precious memories – still being made; the prodding and prayers; the tears and laughter; the gifts and sacrifices.

Thank you my family and friends for helping me in so many ways to get this book out and to keep writing the next chapter of my life...

Foreword

Back to the Basics – Simple Secrets for Living in Victory by **Rev. Toyin Okutinyang** is a fresh and timely reminder to the church that foundational principles cannot be removed, neither do they become obsolete but must be fortified for fruitful Christian living.

A building with a weak or failing foundation cannot support the superstructure. The foundations are not obvious to the naked eye, but without them the building is doomed to give way. The foundational principles are the principles we live by daily, principles practiced daily on which the Christian life and witness stand. When these fundamentals are ignored the Christian witness is compromised and the world does not see Jesus.

The basic principles are the same for all and God is no respecter of persons. A good conscience,

Bible reading, time in prayer, being filled with the Holy Spirit, abiding in a Bible-believing local church, walking in love, contentment, being a true witness at home, speaking the truth and living holy are some of the foundational truths discussed in Back to the Basics.

Toyin delivers a message of hope, that the believer can start over and with the help of the Holy Spirit fortify the foundations that the name of the Lord be glorified.

Rev. Dr. Tunde Bolanta
Overseer, Restoration Ministries Worldwide
Kaduna, Nigeria

Where We Began

ABC's and 123's

No matter how many degrees you acquire, you will still have to use the same 26 letters of the English alphabet that you learned in kinder-garten to write and communicate. Even with a PhD in mathematics, you will still be adding, subtracting, multiplying and dividing. You can never grow beyond your foundational principles – rather, it's upon them that you must build. In fact, often you must fortify your foundation in order to grow to another, higher, level.

Let's go back to the basics and remind ourselves of some essential, elementary, foundational daily principles and practices that must remain in place for us to maintain an effective Christian life and witness. Things we must ensure that we are doing before trying to get into the seemingly more exciting "super-spiritual" stuff!

2 Peter 1:12-13 (PHILLIPS)
I shall not fail to remind you of things like this although you know them and are already established in the truth. I consider it my duty, as long as I live in the temporary dwelling of this body, to stimulate you by these reminders.

Back to the Basics is all about us acting or living out what we claim to believe; what we sing and dance about. It's okay to go to church and sing and shout, and dance and jump till you get the most vigorous workout ever! However, as I've heard it so aptly put before, **no matter how loud you shout or how high you jump, make sure when your feet touch the ground, you walk straight!** That means, after all your dancing and shouting is done, make sure you live right. **Make sure you live a life that conforms to the WORD and not to the WORLD!** Our greatest witness to win the world to Christ is to be Christ-like.

Recent Trends

It's been interesting to observe a certain trend in recent years. Many Christians would much rather hear messages on how to get their sudden breakthrough, be delivered, defeat enemies that are chasing them, and how to get their miracle financial harvest, etc. – than about anything else. Definitely, from time to time, we can and do experience the need for some of these things in our lives, but our preoccupation and our focus should never be on the enemy, what the enemy is doing, or only on how to get things from God.

Much of what believers consider to be the work of the enemy Satan, or the attacks of their human enemies, is nothing more than the work of their own fleshly inclinations. Since the fall of Adam and Eve in the Garden of Eden, it has been the nature of sinful human flesh to shift the blame to someone else rather than take responsibility, repent, and make the necessary changes. Adam blamed God and the woman God gave him for his actions. In turn, Eve blamed the serpent for her actions.

Genesis 3:8-13 (NKJV)

8 And they heard the sound of the Lord God walking in the garden in the cool of the day, and Adam and his wife hid themselves from the presence of the Lord God among the trees of the garden. 9 Then the Lord God called to Adam and said to him, "Where are you?" 10 So he said, "I heard Your voice in the garden, and I was afraid because I was naked; and I hid myself." 11 And He said, "Who told you that you were naked? Have you eaten from the tree of which I commanded you that you should not eat?" 12 **Then the man said, "The woman whom You gave to be with me, she gave me of the tree, and I ate."** *13 And the Lord God said to the woman, "What is this you have done?"* **The woman said, "The serpent deceived me, and I ate."**

Undeveloped Spirits, Unrenewed Minds and Uncontrolled Flesh

Many years ago, the late Bro. Kenneth E. Hagin wrote about how troubled he was by how much carnality he was seeing in the lives of Christians – that is, how much they were ruled by their bodies/flesh and natural appetites. He asked the

Lord, "**Why are there so many carnal Christians?**" The Holy Spirit gave him these **three reasons: undeveloped spirits, unrenewed minds, and uncontrolled flesh**. Indeed, we could preach a month of Sundays on each of these reasons and yet only scratch the surface!

Romans 12:1-2 (NIV)
*1 Therefore, I urge you, brothers and sisters, in view of God's mercy, to **offer your bodies as a living sacrifice, holy and pleasing to God**—this is your true and proper worship. 2 Do not conform to the pattern of this world, **but be transformed by the renewing of your mind**. Then you will be able to test and approve what God's will is—his good, pleasing and perfect will.*

Much of what is preached in the church around us simply appeals to the flesh and our traditional and cultural inclinations. Christianity really is not that complicated. We ministers of the gospel have generally made it harder than it needs to be for God's people. We should be taking our cue from our Lord Jesus who taught so simply and clearly, that even children and the uneducated could understand, eagerly respond, and know what to do.

Basic Rules

Play by The Rules

God created the world and everything in it. He set it all up with order and there's nothing in it that works without rules. Everything around us that runs smoothly is governed by rules. Each sport we play has rules that must be followed for team success. Traffic rules exist to help get us where we need to go on time and keep us safe as we go about our business. Likewise, the Christian life is based on biblical principles for growth and stability that we must adhere to throughout our lives. We never outgrow them or else we will end up making a shipwreck of our faith.

1 Timothy 1:19 (NLT)
Cling to your faith in Christ, and keep your con-

science clear. For some people have deliberately violated their consciences; as a result, their faith has been shipwrecked.

Same Rules for All

In your local church or wherever you fellowship, you will always find yourself amongst believers who have been saved for different lengths of time and who have had different levels of experience with God. No matter how long we've been saved, the same rules apply to both the weathered saint – the 'ancient in the sanctuary', and the new Christian convert.

Where so many of us go wrong is when we start to think that God is a respecter of persons. We think He plays favourites and that because of our special status (prominent ministry position, been saved for a long time, big financial giver, etc.), He will bend the rules for us and overlook our disobedience and sin. **You may be a 'big boy' or a 'big girl' in the eyes of the world, amongst your peers, or even in your church, but you will never be a big boy or girl in the eyes of God!**

It is amazing to see how Christians whom you think should know better, fall into avoidable sin and error. It usually begins unconsciously and starts with the little things, and then it builds over time. They start to think that it doesn't matter if they don't do the things the Bible clearly says they should do. They make excuses for themselves and think they'll get away with it.

1 Corinthians 9:27 (NLT)
I discipline my body like an athlete, training it to do what it should. Otherwise, I fear that after preaching to others I myself might be disqualified.

1 Corinthians 9:27 (MSG)
I don't know about you, but I'm running hard for the finish line. ***I'm giving it everything I've got. No sloppy living for me! I'm staying alert and in top condition. I'm not going to get caught napping, telling everyone else all about it and then missing out myself.***

Let's look at some of the foundational rules of Christian living that have seemed so basic and elementary that many have erroneously thought they could be ignored. The ABC's that have tripped many of us up because we thought we had grown passed them. The same truths we share with new believers apply to those of us who have been saved for many years. We never grow past these things that will keep us on the straight and narrow path to heaven.

1 Corinthians 10:12 (NKJV)
Therefore let him who thinks he stands take heed lest he fall.

Rule 1: Read Your Bible

It really doesn't get much more basic than this, but too many of us just don't do it. We listen to others preach the Bible, sometimes get little bite-size snacks of it here and there, but many have moved away from, or have never even developed a consistent habit of reading the Word for ourselves. Some of us can remember the zeal we had when we first gave our lives to Christ, when we loved to study the Word of God and eagerly share with others what God was showing us in the Bible and speaking to us by His Spirit.

A minister who has enjoyed much success in ministry and prospered in life was asked if there was one thing that he could attribute his success to. He answered that it was the fact that he consistently reads the Bible. Not books about the Bible, devotionals or commentaries (nothing wrong with any of these in themselves), but his priority he said has been to daily feed on the Word. The Bible will meet our every need – give us hope, peace, comfort, joy, wisdom, direction, etc. That is how we feed our spirits.

Psalm 119:11 (NLT)
Your word I have treasured and stored in my heart, that I may not sin against You.

Psalm 119:105 (NLT)
Your word is a lamp to my feet and a light to my path.

1 Peter 2:2 (NKJV)
As newborn babes, desire the pure milk of the Word, that you may grow thereby.

The good old Sunday School song that some of us sang as children, *"Read your Bible, pray every day if you want to grow...",* rings ever true and leads us right into our next *Back to the Basics* rule.

Rule 2: Pray and Talk to God

Praying to God our heavenly Father ought to be so simple that we can't get it wrong. Unfortunately, I think prayer has been made far too complicated for some of us and chased us away from praying for the most part. When we read in the Bible that it was Jesus' practice to get up a great while before daylight to pray or that He prayed all night long, many of us are intimidated and feel that we can't live up to that standard – so why bother at all!

Mark 1:35 (NKJV)
Now in the morning, having risen a long while before daylight, He went out and departed to a solitary place; and there He prayed.

Granted, some Christians are just too lazy to pray. They want results with no effort. Unfortunately for them, things may have to get so tough in their lives that they will eventually run out of options and finally turn to prayer as a last resort! That should never be the case with us.

Let's make prayer simple so that we can all do it. Praying is simply talking to God. It starts with you opening your eyes in the morning and saying, "Thank you Lord for another day. I can see, hear, breathe, I'm alive!" Prayer is offering thanks and gratitude for big and small mercies as you go about your business throughout the day. It has often been said that the highest form of prayer is praise.

Prayer ought to be conversations with God from the moment you get up, during your commute to work, when cooking, cleaning, asking Him what you should do on a project, or how to handle your child's situation, etc. It should be a continuous stream of back-and-forth interaction with God all day long. You shouldn't only pray during your time of devotion or times of specific intercession (which are necessary too), rather praying should involve non-stop communion. That's why I say, **just TALK to God!** Some Christians whose lives have had huge worldwide impact have said **they don't pray long, but they don't go long without praying**. That indeed is the practical way to pray without ceasing.

1 Thessalonians 5:16-18 (NKJV)
[16] Rejoice always, [17] pray without ceasing, [18] in

everything give thanks; for this is the will of God in Christ Jesus for you.

Evidently then from the above verses, **we are out of the will of God when we don't pray, and it will cost us more than we want to pay. If we've become too busy to pray, we're too busy with the wrong things.** If Jesus needed to pray and Paul needed to pray, WE ABOVE ALL need to pray!

Matthew 26:41 (AMP)
Keep actively watching and praying that you may not come into temptation; the spirit is willing, but the body is weak."

The Bible is our guide to a successful prayer life. Before praying about anything, we should find scriptures that speak to our needs or requests, then we pray in line with the Word as a foundation for our prayer.

Rule 3: Be Filled with The Spirit

Jesus Himself, the head of the church, commanded the first believers in Acts 1:4-8 to stay in Jerusalem until they were baptized with the Holy Spirit – the Promise of the Father. On the Day of Pentecost in Acts 2, the Holy Spirit came and filled them, and this infilling was evidenced by them speaking in tongues. Later in that chapter, Peter in his sermon makes it clear that the gift of the Holy Spirit is God's promise to his audience, to those who are far away, and *"as many as the Lord our God will call."* (Acts 2:38-39).

Are you saved? If so, then you are called by the Lord to know Him and live for Him. Jesus' commandment to the first Christians still applies to those of us He has called to Himself today. After giving your life to Jesus, He, the head of the church commands you to move on to the next step, be filled with the Spirit. **The baptism of the Holy Spirit with the evidence of speaking in tongues is the Promise of the Father to every Christian – back then in Acts, today and tomorrow!** The New Testament was written to Spirit-filled believers because all the church was expected to be Spirit-filled.

Too many are endeavouring to live the Christian life without being filled with the Spirit. We earlier learned that one of the reasons for rampant carnality in the body of Christ is failure to develop the human spirit. Receiving the Holy Spirit and learning to follow Him daily are essential to overcoming the problem of an undeveloped spirit. After the initial infilling or baptism of the Holy Spirit, the Bible teaches that we are to develop, train and build up our human spirits, and maintain a Spirit-filled life.

Jude 20-21 (NKJV)
*[20] But you, **beloved, building yourselves up on your most holy faith, praying in the Holy Spirit**, [21] keep yourselves in the love of God, looking for the mercy of our Lord Jesus Christ unto eternal life.*

Ephesians 5:18 (ISV)
*Stop getting drunk with wine, which leads to wild living, but **keep on being filled with the Spirit**.*

Rule 4: Go to Church

There are many reasons why people stop going to church or become 'church dropouts', but none of them are good enough to justify disobeying scripture. For example, some have complained that they can't find any more true Christian churches – they simply haven't looked hard enough! God always has a remnant of true believers even in the midst of quacks and fakes.

You've probably heard this before, but it's a truth that bears repeating. There are no perfect churches and if per chance you found one, the moment YOU joined it, it would cease to be perfect! **All churches are imperfect because they are made up of imperfect people like you and me – imperfect people seeking to know and serve a perfect God.** No matter where in the world you live, you just have to look hard enough and ask God to lead you to a group of those who are worshipping Him in spirit and in truth.

Hebrews 10:25 (AMP)
Not forsaking or neglecting to assemble together

[as believers], as is the habit of some people, but admonishing (warning, urging, and encouraging) one another, and all the more faithfully as you see the day approaching.

The church is Jesus' idea and His creation, not your pastor's. He said "I will build my church..." The epistles were written to local churches, not to individual believers sitting at home because it was the biblical pattern for believers to gather in church and receive the Word of God there. Your internet church and pastor will not sit down and counsel you, visit you in hospital, marry you or dedicate your children. For all of these things to happen, you have to show up physically at a local church where you become a part of that congregation.

Be Careful Where You Worship

Yes you must go to church, but don't just go to ANY church, be careful where you worship. Choose a church with sound biblical teaching and practices. It's only when you regularly feed on the Word of God yourself that you will be able to recognize error and won't just swallow everything you hear. Do not remain under the influence of corrupt, greedy, and immoral leadership, or those with heretical practices. Sin is contagious and evil company does corrupt good morals. Transference of wrong spirits also occurs in such settings and furthermore, you don't want to endorse such ministries by worshipping there.

A lady once approached me to discuss the case of a male relative of hers. This man had become a member of a large church that had branches in many cities around the country. This sister was very concerned about changes in this man's life since he started worshipping in that church. Previously he and his family had been worshipping somewhere else and he'd been growing and doing well, but since joining this new church he gradually started to smoke, drink alcohol and cheat on his wife – things he had never even done as an unbeliever before he became a Christian. This sister wanted to know if it was possible for transference of evil spirits to occur, because it was commonly reported that the pastors and leadership in his new church lived immorally and promiscuously. Absolutely it is possible and it does happen! Furthermore people follow the good or bad example of those who lead them.

1 Corinthians 15:33 (AMP)
*Do not be so deceived and misled! Evil compan-
ionships   (communion,   associations)   corrupt and deprave good manners and morals and
character.*

Even the newest believer has the mighty Holy Spirit living in them and can hear His voice loud and clear. That's why it must grieve the Spirit so much when Christians choose to stay in churches, and under ministry leadership that is engaged in open sin and blatantly unscriptural practices. Many have continued to worship in such places because they see the crowds gathered there and falsely believe that despite the objectionable things they are observing, God must somehow still be in the mix – after all He's blessing the ministry isn't He?! Your continued presence in such places is an endorsement of their wrongdoing and worse still, others over whom you have influence, are liable to follow you there. Do not be deceived. God is far from many places called churches regardless of how large their congregations are, or how many supernatural signs are in manifestation.

Matthew 7:21-23 (NKJV)
21 "Not everyone who says to Me, 'Lord, Lord,' shall enter the kingdom of heaven, but he who does the will of My Father in heaven. *22* **Many will say to Me in that day, 'Lord, Lord, have we not prophesied in Your name, cast out demons in Your name, and done many wonders in Your name?' *23* And then I will declare to them, 'I never knew you; depart from Me, you who practice lawlessness!'**

2 Peter 2 (NLT)
1 But there were also false prophets in Israel, just as there will be false teachers among you. They will cleverly teach destructive heresies and even deny the Master who bought them. In this way, they will bring sudden destruction on themselves. *2* **Many will follow their evil teaching and shameful immorality. And because of these teachers, the way of truth will be slandered. *3* In their greed they will make up clever lies to get hold of your money.** But God condemned them long ago, and their destruction will not be delayed.

Acts 20:28-32 (NLT)
28 "So guard yourselves and God's people. Feed and shepherd God's flock—his church, purchased

with his own blood—over which the Holy Spirit has appointed you as leaders. [29] I know that false teachers, like vicious wolves, will come in among you after I leave, not sparing the flock. [30] ***Even some men from your own group will rise up and distort the truth in order to draw a following.*** [31] ***Watch out!*** *Remember the three years I was with you—my constant watch and care over you night and day, and my many tears for you.* [32] *"And now I entrust you to God and the message of his grace that is able to build you up and give you an inheritance with all those he has set apart for himself.*

Rule 5: Have Christian Friends

Proverbs 27:17 (NLT)
As iron sharpens iron, so a friend sharpens a friend.

This point closely follows from the last one on the importance of going to church. I've observed how many have fallen into the error of isolating themselves from good Christian friends who can speak into their lives, and with whom they can be mutually accountable. Their relationships with other believers are purely superficial and often limited to just sharing jokes, videos and political articles on social media!

It's a sad day for you when there's nobody close enough to you to observe the backward steps you are taking, and nobody who cares enough to say something to you about it. It ought not to be that there's no one in your life that you can talk to about what you're going through and ask them to pray and believe God with you. It's a sad and dangerous place to be in as a Christian, to have separated yourself so far from other believers that you are no longer close enough to anyone for them to SEE what's going wrong with you in areas of your life, and SPEAK into your life. It is the devil's strategy to isolate and attack. Just as in the case of a predator chasing a herd of prey, it is the isolated animal that strays from the herd that becomes an easy target for the predator to destroy.

Be careful whom you associate with. Too many Christians have unfortunately had to learn the hard way that God does not lie – evil company WILL corrupt your good morals (1 Corinthians 15:33). Unbelievers and people who don't live by biblical standards shouldn't be the ones you spend most of your time with. **You will not be the exception, the one that will do this and will still be able to maintain your Christian witness**. When you spend so much time socializing with ungodly friends or co-workers that you start talking and acting like them, then you have ceased to be the light amongst them. Instead of you the believer INFLUENCING them for Jesus, they have now INFECTED you with sin.

Be Your Brother's Keeper

Not only should your friends help you, you in turn should be a blessing to them and look out for them. From the verse below, I want to stress the part about "warning, urging, and encouraging one another."

Hebrews 10:25 (AMP)
*Not forsaking or neglecting to assemble together [as believers], as is the habit of some people, but admonishing (**warning, urging, and encouraging**) one another, and all the more faithfully as you see the day approaching.*

If you see a brother or sister who has developed the habit of not going to church, God expects you to, and you owe it to them, to seek them out and warn, urge and encourage them of the danger they are in if they don't change their ways. This applies not only to those who have stopped fellowshipping with other believers, but to fellow Christians who have missed it in other areas of their lives. I owe it to my brother or sister to warn, urge and encourage them in their faith. We should care enough about each other to obey the following instructions:

Galatians 6:1 (AMP)

Brethren, if any person is overtaken in misconduct or sin of any sort, you who are spiritual [who are responsive to and controlled by the Spirit] should set him right and restore and reinstate him, without any sense of superiority and with all gentleness, keeping an attentive eye on yourself, lest you should be tempted also.

Rule 6: Walk in Love

Valentine's Day is a time of the year when people make a lot of fuss about love so-called. God is love, the real love expert and He has told us what love is all about.

John 15:12-13 (NLT)
*^{12} This is my commandment: Love each other in the same way I have loved you. ^{13} **There is no greater love than to lay down one's life for one's friends.***

We can create the atmosphere of heaven – love – in our homes, workplaces and communities if we purpose to put others first.

1 John 4:19-21 (NLT)
*^{19} We love each other because he loved us first. ^{20} If someone says, "I love God," but hates a fellow believer, that person is a liar; for **if we don't love people we can see, how can we love God, whom we cannot see?** ^{21} And he has given us this command: Those who love God must also love their fellow believers.*

Let Charity (Love) Begin at Home

Your greatest witness is at home. If we want to know what you're really like, we'll have to ask those who live with you. The real me is not the person you interact with socially or see in church for a few hours on Sundays. Most of us have enough self-control to act nice for short periods of time when we present our 'public' face to the world. Go ask my husband and kids, they'll tell you what the real me is like behind closed doors.

What would the people you live with and closely interact with say about how you treat them? How do you treat your spouse when no one else is there? You don't want to be the respected brother at church, who beats up his wife and terrorizes his kids at home. Or the woman of God who unleashes her vicious tongue on her husband outside the public gaze, and who refuses to take care of her home.

James 1:26 (NLT)
If you claim to be religious but don't control your tongue, you are fooling yourself, and your religion is worthless.

Rule 7: Maintain Your Christian Witness

When we stay vitally connected to Jesus the vine, we the branches will bear the fruit that all men will see and know that we are His disciples. Our lives will be a natural overflow of the relationship we maintain or don't maintain with the Lord. Our witness to others is in both what we say and do. I really encourage you to read Ephesians 4:17-32, 5:1-14. Here are some of the verses in which the Bible tells us how to live as children of the light.

Ephesians 4:17, 21-25, 28, 30-32 (NLT)

[17] With the Lord's authority I say this: Live no longer as the Gentiles do, for they are hopelessly confused... [21] Since you have heard about Jesus and have learned the truth that comes from him, [22] throw off your old sinful nature and your former way of life, which is corrupted by lust and deception. [23] **Instead, let the Spirit renew your thoughts and attitudes. [24] Put on your new nature, created to be like God—truly righteous and holy.** *[25] So stop telling lies. Let us tell our neighbors the truth, for we are all parts of the*

same body... [28] If you are a thief, quit stealing. Instead, use your hands for good hard work, and then give generously to others in need... [30] **And do not bring sorrow to God's Holy Spirit by the way you live...** *[31] Get rid of all bitterness, rage, anger, harsh words, and slander, as well as all types of evil behavior. [32] Instead, be kind to each other, tenderhearted, forgiving one another, just as God through Christ has forgiven you.*

Ephesians 5:1-11 (NLT)
[1] **Imitate God, therefore, in everything you do, because you are his dear children.** *[2] Live a life filled with love, following the example of Christ. He loved us and offered himself as a sacrifice for us, a pleasing aroma to God.*

[3] Let there be no sexual immorality, impurity, or greed among you. Such sins have no place among God's people. [4] Obscene stories, foolish talk, and coarse jokes—these are not for you. Instead, let there be thankfulness to God. [5] **You can be sure that no immoral, impure, or greedy person will inherit the Kingdom of Christ and of God. For a greedy person is an idolater, worshipping the things of this world.**

[6] Don't be fooled by those who try to excuse these sins, for the anger of God will fall on all who dis-

obey him. [7] Don't participate in the things these people do. [8] For once you were full of darkness, but now you have light from the Lord. **So live as people of light! [9] For this light within you produces only what is good and right and true.** *[10] Carefully determine what pleases the Lord.* **[11] Take no part in the worthless deeds of evil and darkness; instead, expose them.**

We can't claim to be Christians and then live like unbelievers. I think many have been deceived into thinking that because we are saved by grace and not by works, then no matter what we do after salvation, God will forgive us and we'll be just fine. The following are some areas to take special note of in maintaining your witness as a believer.

How You Live Matters

"Be careful little eyes what you see… little ears what you hear… little feet where you go", is another great song from Sunday School which people my age should still be singing and practicing! Many of us have mistakenly thought we could get away with hours of mindless TV, movie watching and online surfing, and it wouldn't

affect us in any way. Only for some to now find themselves addicted to things like online gambling, all kinds of sexual immorality such as internet porn, sexting, and extra-marital emotional and physical affairs that started through dating websites and apps.

Let's go back to asking ourselves before we watch any movie, surf that internet site, listen to that song, go to that place, etc., **WWJD – What Would Jesus Do?** A few years ago we used to wear jewelry with WWJD on it. Now let's ask ourselves that before we do ANYTHING!

Psalm 101:3 (NLT)
I will refuse to look at anything vile and vulgar... I will have nothing to do with them.

God is not mocked. It's not okay to be fasting, praying and going to all night prayer vigils, yet gossiping, stealing from your employer, robbing orphans and widows, and withholding salaries from your staff while you live in luxury. A single mother who cleaned the houses of several wealthy families told me how some of them would not pay her regularly and would owe her months of pay at a time. Luxury cars were parked in front of these expensive houses, while the owners stepped out in fine clothing on their way to church on Sundays but they refused to pay the humble cleaning lady for the work she'd done!

Likewise, consider the true story of a so-called Christian business man who was prominent in his church. His lavish lifestyle involved jet setting to exotic locations in the world for weekend getaways. One of the senior managerial staff in his large corporate enterprise repeatedly witnessed how he would regularly help himself to the company funds to pay for his weekend partying. All this continued at the same time that contractors who had provided services to his company would go unpaid for many months. This senior manager recounted how his heart broke one day when one of those contractors came pleading and begging to be paid for his work, stating how he could not feed his children or provide for his family's needs.

James 5:4 (MSG)
All the workers you've exploited and cheated cry out for judgment. The groans of the workers you

used and abused are a roar in the ears of the Master Avenger.

Deuteronomy 24:14-15 (NKJV)
14 "You shall not oppress a hired servant who is poor and needy, whether one of your brethren or one of the aliens who is in your land within your gates. 15 Each day you shall give him his wages, and not let the sun go down on it, for he is poor and has set his heart on it; lest he cry out against you to the Lord, and it be sin to you.

Tell the Truth

Develop a trustworthy reputation. It should never be said of us, "You have to take whatever they say with a MOUNTAIN of salt!" We all probably know people that our first reaction to anything they tell us is that it's a lie. Then we have to probe, investigate and fact-check before accepting it. It is deplorable how Christians can boldly lie to your face without batting an eyelid – they know, you know, and God knows they're lying, but they won't back down!

Proverbs 12:22 (AMPC)
Lying lips are extremely disgusting and hateful to

the Lord, but they who deal faithfully are His delight.

1 Peter 3:10-11 (NLT)
[10] For the Scriptures say, "If you want to enjoy life and see many happy days, keep your tongue from speaking evil and your lips from telling lies. [11] Turn away from evil and do good. Search for peace, and work to maintain it.

Keep Your Commitments

Practice excellence and integrity in ALL your dealings and affairs. Go above and beyond what is expected of you; don't just do the barest minimum to get by. Be on time. Develop a reputation for punctuality and keeping your word. Mean exactly what you say and say exactly what you mean. For example, if you volunteer to serve at a task or in an area of ministry, then show up every time like you promised, and serve with all your heart as if you are being paid to do it.

Most of us have probably told someone, "I'll be praying for you." but never did any such thing. We probably had the desire to do so, but for one reason or another, never got around to it or simply forgot. I have developed the habit of saying this instead, **"I'll pray for you when I think of you and remember to."** That I find is more honest and a promise I can keep with a good conscience.

Be Careful with Money

Have you ever been given money to go and buy something but after you purchased it, you didn't give back the full amount of change? You see an opportunity at work to keep a little bit of money back for yourself without anybody knowing and you seize it. Everyone around you is taking bribes in the government office where you work. Now you the 'big sister' in the fellowship that everybody used to look up to have succumbed to the pressure and you're doing the same thing too. After all, you too need extra money to build your own house and pay for your children's school fees!

There's nothing wrong with having money but everything wrong with money having you! Money is a tool that is required to live on earth and a tool that should be used in the right way.

1 Timothy 6:6-10 (NLT)

[6] Yet true godliness with contentment is itself great wealth. [7] After all, we brought nothing with us when we came into the world, and we can't take anything with us when we leave it. [8] So if we have enough food and clothing, let us be content.

[9] But people who long to be rich fall into temptation and are trapped by many foolish and harmful desires that plunge them into ruin and destruction. *[10] For the love of money is the root of all kinds of evil.* **And some people, craving money, have wandered from the true faith and pierced themselves with many sorrows.**

Final Thoughts

Return to The Fear of God

"*Kini* big deal?" (or "What's the big deal?") was imprinted on a t-shirt someone gave my daughter several years ago. I think some of us are wearing that t-shirt by the cavalier attitude we demonstrate towards sin. In our humour and casual talk, we mix scripture and the name of Jesus with profanity and jesting about sin and immorality, and to us it's not a big deal! My brothers and sisters, these things ought not so to be.

Maybe we think God doesn't see or care because people don't. He's still the same God today that exposed Ananias and Sapphira in Acts 5. They dropped dead in church for lying to the Holy

Spirit. In the 1980's, I visited a church in England several times and was told that not too long before then, a group of ministers had met there for their time of fellowship together. During the meeting, they lovingly tried to correct one of them who was involved in some wrongdoing. The fellow was so offended that they would dare to confront him and started to angrily storm out of the building, only to drop dead in the aisle on his way out! May the reverential fear of God that fell on all who heard of the events of Acts 5 and that English church, fall on us too today!

2 Corinthians 7:1 (NIV)
Therefore, since we have these promises, ***dear friends, let us purify ourselves from everything that contaminates body and spirit, perfecting holiness out of reverence for God.***

There Is Hope

"The reason the world is not seeing Jesus is that Christian people are not filled with Jesus. They are satisfied with attending meetings weekly, reading the Bible occasionally, and praying sometimes. It is an awful thing for me to see people who profess to be Christians lifeless, powerless, and in a place

where their lives are so parallel to unbelievers' lives that it is difficult to tell which place they are in, whether in the flesh or in the Spirit."
– Smith Wigglesworth

Financial pressure, work pressure, peer pressure, school challenges, health challenges, family pressures from trying to raise and support a family, the list goes on – the stuff of life. Such have become your excuse to make one compromise after another. Now you're doing things that a few years back you could never have imagined that you as a Christian would ever be involved in. You lie readily. You take and give bribes. You cheat and take what does not belong to you. Online chat rooms. Internet pornography. Flirting in the workplace. Now you've committed fornication or adultery in your heart and even progressed to it in your actions.

When separation and isolation from godly influence lead people down the path of progressive sin, the problem is further compounded by the resulting shame and pride that then makes them hide and deny their true state.

We have already noted that there are so many carnal Christians because of **undeveloped spirits, unrenewed minds and uncontrolled flesh**. Thank God however, each of us can do something to change that in our own lives. There's no need to despair. No matter where we may have been missing it, the GOOD NEWS is that we can repent and start over!

Never Too Late

We should never fall for Satan's lie that we've gone too far and there's no way we can go back to our first love. **Why save face in front of people, all those who've been looking up to you as a big boy/girl, but lose face before God?!** "How can I let them know I have a problem? People look up to me. I can't let anyone know I've missed it."

I encourage you to follow the example of King David in the Old Testament and become a man/woman after God's heart – one who is quick to admit and confess, and quick to repent and run back to the Lord. Reject the path of King Saul who on the other hand, did the exact opposite. He blamed others for his sins and ended up being completely rejected by God. God loves us so much and according to 1 John 1:9, if we confess our sins, He is faithful and just to cleanse us from ALL unrighteousness.

1 John 1:7-10 (NKJV)
^{7} But if we walk in the light as He is in the light, we have fellowship with one another, and the blood of Jesus Christ His Son cleanses us from all sin. ^{8} If we say that we have no sin, we deceive ourselves, and the truth is not in us. ^{9} If we confess our sins, He is faithful and just to forgive us our sins and to cleanse us from all unrighteousness. ^{10} If we say that we have not sinned, we make Him a liar, and His word is not in us.

What if the prodigal son in Luke 15 had said, "I've strayed too far to go back home!"? He would have died in his sins. We're seeing the prodigal son here as a type of the backslidden Christian who is restored to a loving relationship with God the Father – not as a sinner who never knew God and who is giving His life to Christ for the first time.

Luke 15:17-24 (NKJV)
^{17} "But when he came to himself, he said, 'How

many of my father's hired servants have bread enough and to spare, and I perish with hunger! [18] *I will arise and go to my father, and will say to him, "Father, I have sinned against heaven and before you,* [19] *and I am no longer worthy to be called your son. Make me like one of your hired servants."'*

[20] *"And he arose and came to his father. But when he was still a great way off, his father saw him and had compassion, and ran and fell on his neck and kissed him.* [21] *And the son said to him, 'Father, I have sinned against heaven and in your sight, and am no longer worthy to be called your son.'*

[22] *"But the father said to his servants, 'Bring out the best robe and put it on him, and put a ring on his hand and sandals on his feet.* [23] *And bring the fatted calf here and kill it, and let us eat and be merry;* [24] *for this my son was dead and is alive again; he was lost and is found.' And they began to be merry.*

Don't be too proud to admit that you need help; that you've strayed; that you need godly friends to be accountable to; that you need to repent and ask for God's forgiveness. Admit it to yourself, admit it to God, admit it to those you've wronged, and admit it someone who can minister to you and help restore you. Don't be too proud to say "I'm sorry" to those you've hurt. **Saying "I'm sorry" and "I was wrong" won't kill you; instead, it will give you new life and set you free.** It will heal your broken relationships with God and with the people in your life. The prodigal son in the Bible did just that and his story ended beautifully. Don't you want your life story to end beautifully too?

Finally...

Philippians 4:8-9 (ESV)
8 Finally, brothers, whatever is true, whatever is honorable, whatever is just, whatever is pure, whatever is lovely, whatever is commendable, if there is any excellence, if there is anything worthy of praise, think about these things. 9 What you have learned and received and heard and seen in me—practice these things, and the God of peace will be with you.

Let us all continue to shore up our foundations and ensure that we are sound in basic principles of Christian living. My prayer and hope is that as we are nurtured in the Word, we will go on to daily demonstrate the character of Christ. And by so doing, may it be said of us as it was of the early believers in Acts 17:6, that we too have turned our worlds upside down for Jesus!

Jude 24-25 (NKJV)
[24] *Now to Him who is able to keep you from stumbling, and to present you faultless before the presence of His glory with exceeding joy,* [25] *To God our Savior, who alone is wise, be glory and majesty, dominion and power, both now and forever. Amen.*

Prayer of Salvation

If you would like to receive Jesus Christ as your Saviour and Lord, please pray this from your heart:

Heavenly Father, I come to You in the name of Jesus. You said in Your Word that if I confess with my mouth that "Jesus is Lord" and believe in my heart that God raised Him from the dead, I will be saved (Romans 10:9-10).

I believe with my heart that Jesus is the Son of God and I believe He was raised from the dead for my justification. Right now I call on the name of Jesus and declare that He is my Lord! Thank You Lord for forgiving me of my sins and delivering from the power of darkness and dominion of Satan over my life.

Thank You Lord, I AM SAVED!

NEXT STEPS

Congratulations on making this life changing decision and welcome to the family of God!

Please email us or contact us online as we'd love to hear that you've made this decision.

To grow in your new Christian life, review and follow the principles shared in this book. Jesus loves you and has a wonderful plan for you – your best days are ahead in Him!